CU00641627

SECOND EDITION

Skomer Memories © 2017 by Geoffrey Codd
Printed by Print Team (Dorset) Ltd
ISBN 978-1-5272-1273-2

All rights reserved. No part of this publication
may be reproduced in any form without prior
permission of the copyright owner.

Named participants in this story are family
members and much respected members of a
village community who supported our island
endeavours in many ways.

Photographs from the period 1934 to 1950
were taken from the Codd Family Album. The
Puffin group on the front cover was kindly
contributed by Mike Alexander (who, together
with his wife Rosanne, spent ten happy years
on Skomer as Warden in the 1970/80s). Other
photographs provided by courtesy of Mike
Alexander and Rachel Mullett - Pembrokeshire
Moments, as attributed.

James and Kate

I hope that you enjoy this one

Geoff and Christine

SKOMER MEMORIES

A story of the trials, tribulations, and joys experienced by the last family to own and farm this enchanting island

With my deepest thanks to my wife Christine
for all her painstaking work in editing this story and
in asking the right questions to revive old memories.

I also share these memories with my sisters
June and Valerie who I hope will enjoy these
reminders of our many happy years growing up on
Skomer. We also shared the sadness when
we left our beloved island home for the last time.

My thanks also to the Wildlife Trust of South and
West Wales who kindly provided a rare opportunity
to rekindle vivid memories of our family's life
on Skomer during some very challenging times.

Preface

This story starts on a sunny day in 1922 when my grandmother Cecilia Sturt was in London meeting friends and indulging in a little shopping. Life was good for Cecilia and Walter Sturt, a retired dentist of some renown, and their only child Betty. They were looking forward to a relaxing retirement enjoying their new holiday home in Dawlish, the heart of what was then regarded as the English Riviera, and to making more use of their new motor launch 'Dixie'.

On that day in London, while Cecilia was killing time between appointments and doing a little window shopping, she came across the London office of Knight Frank & Rutley the estate agents. Idly glancing at what was currently available, as one does, she noticed that Lord Kensington in Pembrokeshire was disposing of some of his estate - four islands, together with some adjacent coastline and a house on the mainland.

On little more than a whim, my Grandmother decided that it would be nice to own some islands - and thus the scene was set for a life that would be so different from normal expectations. In their new Pembrokeshire home, Betty would eventually meet and fall in love with Reuben Codd, the youngest son of a local farmer, and these two young people, from such widely different backgrounds, would elope to get married. Their first child June was born in 1931, I was born in 1932 and my young sister Valerie arrived in 1936 to complete the family.

Life for the Codd family on Skomer island was delightful in so many ways, but also deeply demanding and challenging. Nature seemed to throw every impediment in their way, and it was a constant battle to overcome each challenge. However, their dogged determination, and the sheer magic of living in such a place, gave them the strength to persevere against all the odds to build an island family life that many would give their eye teeth for.

The following story is about how that family promoted Skomer

The young Codd family in 1935 - the year before Valerie was born.

as a place for wildlife lovers to visit, while at the same time trying to make a living out of farming whilst still protecting the island's unique habitat. Achieving these often competing objectives was quite a challenge for two people who had come from widely different backgrounds and upbringings, and who both held very different views on what was important in life. Moreover, both had very strong personalities which amplified those differences.

The promotion of Skomer as a unique wildlife habitat was a cause that was very close to Mother's heart. On the other hand it was the farming challenge, and at the same time protecting Skomer's unique habitat, that was Fathers driving force. However, each of these challenges provided numerous opportunities to create common ground between them; each loved their island home very much and had a shared resolve to preserve and enhance it. It has to be said though that, as the years passed, their widely differing expectations from life gradually made family cohesion increasingly difficult to sustain.

Mother was an only child and was just twelve years old when her parents bought Skomer and the other islands. She was undoubtedly quite a headstrong child, used to getting her own way, and was certainly used to experiencing the finer things of life. On the other hand she was happy to work very hard to achieve her aims, and was a practical and imaginative woman who relished a challenge - both of those attributes being supremely important in making a success of family life on Skomer.

Father's background could not have been more different. My paternal grandfather had been a mill owner who had moved into farming at East Hook farm near Marloes early in the twentieth century, when farmers started to install oil engines to grind their corn, thereby replacing their dependence on the old water mills.

Father was the youngest of twelve children who were all expected to help with farm chores - often at the expense of their education – and he had a tough upbringing by a 'God fearing' father who believed in applying strong discipline. This tough formative experience of farming life at the sharp end, together with his natural country skills such as rabbit harvesting, could not have been a better preparation for dealing with many of the farming challenges on Skomer island.

East Hook Farm where Father was born and where he learned his farming skills - painted in 1918 by a billeted WW1 soldier, Private Hoddinot.

Indeed, in those days to be farming at East Hook farm was almost as remote as being on an island. The county town of Haverfordwest was over fifteen miles away, and Father often had to undertake that return journey on market-day by horse and cart - a very long working day by the time that one returned home. We tend to forget just how basic life was before the introduction of motorised transport for the many, particularly in the rural communities.

Like Mother, Father also had a very strong personality. His was grounded in his devout Baptist upbringing which formed a very important part of his life. Chapel attendance in Marloes village was always important to him, although living on Skomer with its vagaries of weather meant that chapel attendance was somewhat irregular. He also had a very strong work ethic and was a powerful man physically, essential attributes for tackling the Skomer challenge.

One surprising deficiency in that context was that he could not swim a stroke. He always claimed that it meant that he would never take any risks in rough weather, but I have to say that I never observed any hesitation whatsoever when setting out in the most threatening of weather conditions!

Finally however it was the clash of those widely different personalities, as well as the relentless grind of the island farming challenge, which brought my parents to the point where they decided that there just had to be a separation of the ways. They therefore decided that there was simply no option but to sell their beloved island home and go their separate ways. That is where this story ends and a new era began for us all.

In the following pages I have set out to recapture some of the ups and downs of the Codd family's life on Skomer over three decades. That life exposed many challenges for the family, including during the WW2 years when Father's HM Coastguard responsibilities meant that the island had to be managed remotely.

A high level of extemporisation and resourcefulness were essential attributes when dealing with some of those island challenges, where easily accessible outside support was non-existent. Today, that life would be so different from those far off days; Air/Sea Rescue and new communications technologies have transformed the lives of people in remote places.

There were many occasions when immense reserves of courage and faith in oneself were called for in the face of those challenges, and island life also laid bare one's human frailties all too easily. But, in spite of all that, the overpowering magic of life in such a place cannot fail to totally captivate the spirit and make life so worthwhile and rewarding.

A very special place

What is it that makes an island such a very special place? No doubt the sense of remoteness from the everyday trials and tribulations of the world outside is part of its attraction, a sense of remoteness that is constantly reinforced through the sight of the surrounding sea and its obvious ability to shape one's life for good or ill. Father repeatedly reminded me that the sea is a really good servant but a very bad master – how true that is.

But for many, an island's attraction is often much more than that. The unique mix of the geology, the wildlife, the landscape, and the human story of achievement - often in very difficult circumstances, all combine to stimulate sensations that can be utterly enthralling and captivating - a different world.

Skomer in the Spring – a vivid display of Bluebells and pink Campion for as far as the eye can see - the spectacle is breathtaking and the perfume completely envelopes you (Photo by courtesy of Mike Alexander).

Skomer is undoubtedly a very special place. Its fascinating wildlife seems to have been a constant backdrop to life on this enchanting island over the ages, and it is now a bird sanctuary of world renown. This is partly due no doubt to the fact that it is completely vermin free. During the breeding season over 50,000 Puffins, Guillemots and Razorbills, together with over 300,000 Manx Shearwaters - the world's largest colony - provide a sight and a sound that completely takes over one's senses and sensibilities. An experience not to be forgotten. Skomer was scheduled as an Ancient Monument in 1979.

Now imagine that you actually own that island, where that unique mix is deeply embedded in your everyday life. If you then move away, a deep void is left that is never quite filled. That is how I, and my sisters June and Valerie, feel about Skomer island, which was our home during our most formative years. The almost overpowering scent of the bluebells in the Spring, the raucous clamour of thousands of sea birds during the breeding season, the seals defending their pups, and the absolute tranquillity that can descend when all of that is over - that was our much loved family home.

But that was only a part of our island life. The winter months produced a very different and more challenging backdrop to our lives. Strong and often extremely damaging gales were relatively routine during the winter months, producing mountainous seas which battered the shoreline and were a constant threat to the safety of our boats - our only lifeline with the mainland. Even though the Winter challenges called for greater resilience and stoicism, the effort expended in coping with the dangers and discomfort brought a great sense of achievement and personal satisfaction.

Turbulent seas battering Skomer's cliffs - a frequent occurrence during the long Winter months. This picture brings back sharp memories of the sheer wrenching force of that biting wind, with the freezing driving spume whipped up from the water stinging one's face, and numbing one's hands.

A little bit of history

My grandfather, a retired dentist, had bought Skomer, Grassholm, Midland and Gateholm islands from Lord Kensington when his estate was broken up in the early 1920s. Gateholm sits along the coast at one end of Marloes sands, and is only an island at high tide. Midland island sits between Skomer and the mainland and has little to attract visitors, although my sisters and some friends camped there on occasion. Grassholm sits ten miles out in the Atlantic beyond Skomer, and is host to one of the largest colonies of gannets in the world.

The gannet colony on their nests on Grassholm. They have a wingspan of six feet, but clearly don't believe in wasting space. In very hot weather the island can be more than a bit smelly when approached from downwind!

Skomer is by far the largest of the four islands at just under one thousand acres. It is a sea bird sanctuary of considerable note, and has been inhabited on-and-off since Neolithic times. There had been many tenant farmers of the island over the centuries, but our family were the first – and last - owners of the island to commit their lives to protecting its heritage whilst also striving to make a living from its fertile land.

Whilst its land was indeed highly fertile, and its surrounding waters rich in marine life, exploiting those advantages came at an extraordinarily high financial and personal cost. It was in the early 1930's, after their runaway marriage, that my father and mother took up the challenge of farming Skomer, and facilitating special studies of the flora and fauna that are unique to the island - such as the Skomer vole.

They were always particularly keen to welcome research studies by the University of Wales at Aberystwyth, and other naturalists who were fascinated by Skomer's unique features. One unsuccessful experiment was when a pair of Golden Eagles were brought to Skomer to see if they would settle there and breed.

Ubiquitous Puffins on Skomer. Fortunately there is a profusion of rabbit burrows throughout the island, which provide a ready home for these characterful birds.

Skomer's craggy cliffs seemed to hold promising possibilities as a suitable terrain for these majestic birds. For a while it looked as though the gamble would pay off, until there was a particularly bad winter gale. One of the Golden Eagles was never seen again, although the other was said to have been spotted later on Ramsey island ten miles away across St Brides bay.

Guillimot on egg - on a ledge in Skomer North Haven - the egg is shaped such that it will not roll off the ledge.

The farming challenge that Father and Mother faced was considerable. Potato crops lost their premium due to the delays implicit in picking and bringing the crop to market from a remote island. The sacks of 'early' potatoes had to be manhandled off the field by pickers who had to be transported to Skomer from the mainland, involving extra cost and delay. The sacks of potatoes were then taken by horse and dray down to the beach where they were further manhandled down to the water, loaded into the boat, and taken across the Jack Sound to Martins Haven beach.

There they had to be manhandled yet again and carried up the beach to waiting lorries for transport to the market.

And after all of that huge effort, delay, and cost, to then discover that the market was flooded with 'early' potatoes which were by then worth little if anything. Transport of the superbly fattened livestock on Skomer's ultra-verdant vegetation also needed extra labour to be brought from the mainland to help to facilitate that difficult crossing in an open boat. The cards were always heavily stacked against commercial success.

And so it was that in 1950 my family gave up the unequal struggle. Our lovely island home was sold to Mr Leonard Lee, a West Midlands industrialist, and my father and mother divorced and went their separate ways. Both loved the island very much, but the ever constant hard grind of island life had taken its toll. Moreover, they had long had a somewhat tempestuous relationship, driven by different expectations of life, and a parting of the ways was inevitable.

The family breakup was painful, and the loss of our beloved island home made it doubly so for all of us - it created a deep sense of sadness and nostalgia that has stayed with me and my sisters to this day. Since those days though, we have all moved on with our busy lives. For me, revisiting our island home was too painful to contemplate - I felt, wrongly perhaps, that one should never go back, because many of those things that one held dear would inevitably have been changed. But life moves on, and little did I know that an opportunity that I could not possibly ignore would eventually present itself - albeit some sixty five years after my family had sold our wonderful island home.

An opportunity
presents itself

And so it was, on a day in April 2015, that my sister Valerie telephoned to say that our 84 year old elder sister June was to be awarded her Honours degree at Swansea University in July. My wife Christine and I decided that we just had to be there to support her on the big day, and thus it was that the idea of combining a family celebration of her great achievement with a family visit to our beloved Skomer began to take shape. It was a perfect opportunity for my children and grandchildren to see that wonderful place where my sisters and I had grown up.

I contacted Rob Pickford, Chairman of the trustees of the Wildlife Trust of South and West Wales (WTSWW), the guardians of Skomer Island on behalf of Natural Resources Wales, to ask if a private family visit to Skomer could be arranged. This would not only be a nostalgic and emotional visit down memory lane, but would also be a great opportunity to be reassured that our much loved island home is now being cared for and protected in a manner that enables many to enjoy what we took for granted.

Rob and the WTSWW management and staff were kindness itself, and organised a private boat trip across to Skomer, together with personal attention to our needs at every stage of our visit. In spite of very uncertain weather conditions leading up to the day of our visit, the day itself dawned bright and sunny. It turned out to be an absolutely fabulous day throughout - such a happy coincidence of perfect conditions and moving memories. Our only regret was that our son Justin, and his family, were unable to experience this memorable day with us. He had incurred a foot injury just prior to our visit, and this would have made walking on Skomer's rough terrain impossible without endangering his recovery. Such a disappointment.

What follows here is the story of that visit, with a series of pictures and reminiscences on what life on Skomer was really like for the last family to farm it.

The start of a memorable day

On our way to the boat at Martins Haven - John Reynolds' 'Dale Princess' - we had to pass through Marloes village which was our first trigger of childhood memories. After stopping briefly to visit my grandparents' grave near the church gate, it soon became very evident that this village was no longer the working village that had been a part of our childhood – it now appeared to be a gentrified destination for holidaymakers. It seemed that the heart and soul of the old community that we knew so well had clearly gone for ever.

Looking west from a colourful Deer Park towards Skomer, with Midland isla
flowing calmly South, and the farmhouse on Skomer can just be discerned c

Father had always been really close to this community. He and his brothers and sisters had attended the village school towards the end of WW1, when it was run by the headmaster's wife while her husband was away at war, and he had therefore maintained a number of good friendships in the village. This certainly stood him in good stead when he needed help on Skomer to deal with those situations that called for extra manpower.

Even though he was living on Skomer, Father was often called upon to be Master of Ceremonies at the annual Marloes village fete, and to participate in village activities. He also played cricket for the village team and was considered to be a fine batsman. An added bonus for the village were those occasions

...tervening and Wooltack Point in the foreground. The Spring tide can be seen ...e horizon. (Photo by courtesy of Rachel Mullett - Pembrokeshire Moments)

Martins Haven Cottage - our mainland base during the war years. The 10 foot high Deer Park wall in the foreground is a reminder of the Deer Park's relatively recent past.

when Grandfather would join him to play in the village team - he had been a highly experienced Home Counties cricketer.

During the summer months the local sporting events were a regular attraction for us as a family. It was not unusual to bring over from Skomer our pony Billy for June to ride at the local gymkhanas or Point-to-Point in Dale. Mother would also borrow a very fast cob from Archie Thomas at West Hook farm and, despite a heavy handicap, she usually won her races quite spectacularly.

Marloes village was home to the fishermen who kept their boats at Martins Haven, and to local farming families and their agricultural workers. In our day it had a Post Office with a shop in the village square, run by Affie and Peggy Johns who also sold hardware on the other side of the road. I well remember the wonderment in 1948 when they installed a petrol pump – which in those days was operated manually using a long pump handle on the side of the cabinet.

Further up the village on the left there was also Emma's little shop, which sold some tinned food and cigarettes, etc.. Emma was always in a wheel chair and it was unusual for us to pass by on foot without dropping in for a chat. On the other side of the road, just before Emma's shop, lived Jack Edwards a local fisherman and a good friend of Father. Jack was a great help to my family when they were dealing with the early challenges of building a new life on Skomer. But more on Jack later.

Just a few doors up from Jack's home was the village blacksmith. He provided an absolutely essential service to this agricultural and fishing community. A major task for the 'smithie', in addition to the many agricultural wrought ironwork tasks for the local farming community, was the shoeing of horses. Father decided however that, in order to save the time and disruption involved in transport to the mainland, he would set up his own forge facility on Skomer. After quickly brushing up on the

Cutting our hay crop during the war years. The reciprocating cutting bar - on the right hand side - was a great advance over the earlier scythe, with most of the effort now being expended by horses rather than humans.

required 'smithie' skills, he was soon able to shoe our horses on the island as well as carrying out numerous other essential wrought iron tasks.

I well remember Father telling me that the old Marloes Smithie was a heavy pipe smoker who smoked extra strong 'shag' tobacco in an old fashioned white clay pipe - which of course turned a dirty black from continuous use. As was not uncommon in those days he also chewed tobacco, a favourite brand being 'Twist' which was bought in long lengths, a bit like liquorice sticks. This life style did not stop the old Smithie living to the ripe old age of 94!

Continuing on our journey today from Marloes to Martins Haven we passed 'Treehill' and 'East Hook' farms - both of which in my youth had been occupied by my uncles and aunts and their families - and eventually reached Martins Haven car park. The car park takes up a corner of what used to be our cultivated field at the back of our mainland home, Martins Haven Cottage, now called Rath Cottage (the change of name no doubt influenced by the imposing iron-age earthworks on the Deer Park opposite).

During the WW2 years we had temporarily moved out from Skomer to live in this cottage. Although we still spent much time on the island, Martins Haven and the Deer Park was our home stamping ground over that period, and this part of our lives also has many memories for me and my sisters. Life on the mainland was naturally easier in many ways - we grazed animals on the Deer Park, grew some crops nearby, and Father was in charge of the Coastguard Station at Wooltack Point up on the Deer Park.

The island was a sanctuary from everyday wartime life over that period, but on the mainland the evidence of war was everywhere, even in this remote part of the country. On the eastern boundary of Martins Haven cottage, for example, there was the end of a decoy airfield runway's landing lights. This was intended to attract the attention of the German bombers from the real airfield at Dale, from which a 'Free Polish Squadron' of Wellington bombers operated. Fortunately for us, the German bombers ignored it on their many sorties to blitz Swansea, and I can still remember vividly the deep red glow from that burning city sixty miles away, lighting up the sky at night after each bombing raid over three long consecutive nights.

And only a few hundred yards in the other direction, above Martins Haven cove and not far from Ronald Lockley's bungalow (now called Lockley Lodge), was an army searchlight battery and anti-aircraft gun emplacement. Wartime activities were all around us, even in the home.

I walked into our sitting room one day to see a wooden chest with a Tommy-Gun inside - I recognised it as such from American gangster movies that I had seen in the cinema in Haverfordwest. Later on, a Lee-Enfield .303 rifle was added to our arms list. Winston Churchill's declaration that 'we would fight them on the beaches' was not simply empty rhetoric! It is certainly hard to imagine that heightened wartime atmosphere as we park today in that quiet and well-ordered car park.

A Marloes fisherman - Dickie Edwards - about to make a withie lobster pot. The special stand, with holes in the top, enables the neck of the lobster pot to be formed at the start of the construction process. The withies are then gradually bent outwards and downwards (held by the cords at the bottom) to form the sides of the pot, with the bottom of the pot being formed at the end after removing it from the stand.

A growing sense of anticipation

After an enthusiastic welcome by WTSWW staff we walked down towards Martins Haven beach, passing our old garages, now Public Conveniences. Those garages had originally been two cottages that were meant for the use of fishermen, and it is also believed that expectant mothers from the islands were brought there for their confinement.

It was a previous tenant of Skomer - J J Neale - who in about 1905 converted the right hand cottage into a garage to house one of the earliest automobiles in Pembrokeshire. In our day however those garages had also served as a workshop for the servicing of our outboard engines, and for many other such jobs. I remember helping father to make a lobster pot there, using withies pulled from the Deer Park stream nearby. These were shaped using a special wooden stand that he had made for that purpose.

We arrived at the top of the beach approach and it was sad to see that the many fishing boats that used to cram the beach were no longer there. Nor were there any of the lobster pots awaiting their owners' attention, or the lobster storage chests that used to float just off the shore.

Those Marloes fishermen were a tough and resourceful breed, and were always happy to help in times of need. Amongst them was Jack Edwards - of whom more later - and one of my favourites, Harvey Warlow, whose technologically advanced and beautifully engineered 4 stroke Watermota outboard engine was much envied by Father. There was also Dicky Edwards who always had a joke ready and was a dab hand at lobster pot construction (see photo opposite). And it was Freddie Morris who left a very rude message scratched on his boat's oars when his boat had been interfered with in his absence. Colourful characters now long gone.

Unlike the wonderful weather of that day, Martins Haven beach could be particularly exposed when the winds were northerly. During such times the journey to Skomer could be extremely hazardous, if not impossible. On one occasion, when the family had just returned from the usual weekly shopping trip to Haverfordwest, we found one of our boats being washed off the beach in an unexpectedly fierce winter's gale. I still vividly remember how a really vicious undertow of pebbles grabbed at my ankles and almost completely swept me away as we struggled to save the boat. It was only after a considerable struggle that we eventually managed to save it. Such experiences are of course all a part of a working island life.

Whilst waiting for the Skomer boat on that July day, other memories flooded in. I remember helping my father with various boat maintenance jobs on that beach; one such occasion was when several boat timbers needed to be replaced, and the new timbers had to be thoroughly steamed before they could be fitted. Island life develops self-reliance and ingenious extemporisation, and it was certainly so in this case.

Arriving back at Martins Haven - our embarkation point for Skomer. One can just spot another boat load of visitors for Skomer embarking off Martins Haven beach.

Many Marloes fishing boats still operated out of Martins Haven in the 1940s and 50s - note the winches in the foreground that were used to pull boats over greased timbers, placed at intervals in front of the boat as it was pulled forward up the beach.

Father found a piece of old iron pipe, bunged a large piece of cork in the end, put some water in the bottom, leaned it up against a rock at an angle, and lit a fire under it. In this way the timber inserted into the pipe steamed thoroughly, thereby allowing perfect shaping to the curve of the boat's planking. I particularly remember this occasion because the pipe slipped off the rock and hit me on the head, throwing me to the ground. (My wife Christine says that that explains a lot!)

There were many other memories of this beach, of those summer days when we would take dozens of nature lovers of all ages across to Skomer in our open boats, which were propelled by a small outboard engine. A spare engine was always carried in case of any unexpected mishap (such as losing an engine off the stern of the boat, which did happen on at least one occasion).

On really calm days the surface of the water would be as smooth as glass, and one could clearly discern the myriad of life

Father leaving Skomer North Haven. Note the ever present spare 'Seagull' outboard engine, and the essential toolbox that happens to provide a more comfortable seat. And his trousers, as usual, wet below the knee from repeated immersion in sea water when launching off the beach.

on the seabed - an absolute delight. And sometimes, as evening was closing in, we would take friends out in the boat to fish close under the cliffs. The prize would be a good catch of a dozen pollock or mackerel for our supper.

Waiting on today's walkway at Martins Haven to embark on the Dale Princess.

And so to the Island at last

The journey to Skomer today is very different indeed. There is now a walkway, built out over the rock promontory on the left side of Martins Haven bay, which ends at a point where the Dale Princess can safely embark passengers for the island. It works well, and one couldn't help thinking how much easier it was doing it this way – although one still couldn't help missing that closer exposure to the elements that was always a part of our much smaller open boat experience!

We duly set off for Skomer and, as we passed Wooltack Point, we could see the strong tide flow heading west. Anyone familiar with the Jack Sound tide race could not fail to anticipate a rough passage through the Sound if it was travelling North – but fortunately for us today the nearly top-of-the-tide westerly direction meant that it was relatively calm on this occasion. Sadly, though, today we did not see any sign of the porpoises that often used to escort us on our passage through the Jack Sound.

I particularly remember one occasion when, with a boat full of visitors, someone spotted a little black blob on the horizon. It seemed to be headed for Ireland in the strong westerly tide, so we thought that perhaps we should investigate. Eventually, and much to our surprise, we saw that it was a man in swimming trunks, in what appeared to be a giant tyre inner tube. It turned out to be an airman from the nearby base at Dale, who had gone to sleep and floated out to sea in an aircraft inner tube. He was too frightened by the tide race in the Jack Sound to leave the tube and was saying his last prayers when we spotted him. I don't know which he found the worst - his frightening experience, or the fact that the Camp Commander was on our boat at the time!

There was a less welcome encounter in the Jack Sound during the wartime years, when one of our passengers spotted something on the horizon which eventually became recognisable as a mine that had obviously broken loose from its underwater

A strong tide going west today as we passed Little Sound on our way to Skomer.

moorings. As the manacing object floated past in the strong current, literally only a few yards from us, we could clearly see the long copper spikes that housed the detonators, and I am sure that I was not the only one to feel that nervous tingling up my spine until we had left it safely behind us. It was of course reported soon afterwards so that it could be detonated by rifle fire.

As we passed Midland island today it was not difficult to identify the spot where the SS Lonsdale had foundered in a ferocious gale in October 1938 - as did the SS Mosely only eleven years previously with the loss of six crew members, and that of the First Officer's wife on almost the same spot. In 1938, our father, mother and grandfather had braved the stormy conditions to rescue the crew of the Lonsdale.

The rescue of the crew of the SS Lonsdale - another Jack Sound casualty

It had been just after 6pm on 23rd October 1938 when there was a loud knock on the door of Martins Haven Cottage. Due to the rapidly deteriorating weather conditions Father had just initiated a coastguard 'watch', and my uncle Jim - who was a volunteer watchman - was already on his way from Treehill Farm. Father opened the door to see two bedraggled walkers standing huddled outside the porch in the driving rain. "It looks as though there's a ship in desperate trouble over near the islands" said one. His companion added "There are sounds like banging doors and it looks very odd".

Father quickly donned his oilskin coat and sou'wester and headed for the Coastguard Look-out at Wooltack Point. On arrival there he could just discern, through the driving rain, the blurred shape of a ship with all lights ablaze. She was clearly in some distress close under the cliffs of Midland Island, and he knew immediately who must be in trouble out there. Only a few hours earlier that afternoon, the SS Lonsdale had called at Martins Haven to take on more coal for her boilers. She was on her way from Ireland to Milford Haven and had run her fuel perilously low.

With gale force winds expected imminently, and the barometer dropping rapidly, Captain John Hegarty had thought it prudent to replenish his fuel bunkers at Martins Haven, in spite of the difficulty of doing this in mid-voyage, and off a pebble beach with no loading facilities. Father had telephoned the local coal merchant in Dale village who readily agreed to deliver two loads of coal. This was considered by Captain Hegarty to be just about sufficient to reach Milford Haven. The coal eventually arrived and was then laboriously transported out to the SS Lonsdale from Martins Haven beach using the ship's one and only small lifeboat.

Father and Mother had seen the Lonsdale and her crew off safely after the refuelling. Despite the deteriorating weather conditions the Captain had seemed unworried. It transpired however that only a short time after setting sail he realised that the winds were rising faster than he expected. He knew that he still had to head out westwards for the open sea, past Midland Island and around Skomer Head, before being able to head east again along the coast towards eventual shelter in Milford Haven harbour.

A possible, although more hazardous, alternative to this long and circuitous course was to take a short cut between the mainland and Midland Island. This would mean having to negotiate the notorious Jack Sound, with its jagged rocks and its many whirlpools and foaming tide race. However, even this prospect suddenly seemed more attractive than having to battle through the increasingly vicious looking seas that could be observed around the distant Skomer Head.

Many a ship's skipper has had to agonise over just such a decision. The Captain of the Lonsdale was only too conscious of the fact that he had only taken on just enough coal to make harbour at Milford Haven. He reasoned that the shorter journey through the Jack Sound would be preferable to a long drawn out struggle around Skomer with the strong likelihood of running out of fuel once again. Accordingly he turned to port and started to head South into the treacherous tide race which formed the Jack Sound.

The Jack Sound was racing North at about 8-9 knots and the seas were rolling through in a turbulent stream with the gale force winds now cutting across the tide race. The seas and the wind battered the elderly vessel remorselessly as she struggled onwards and the Captain was thankful that at least the daylight should hold out until they reached less dangerous waters. They slowly struggled past the 'Tusker' rock on their port side. This was the first of several jagged granite outcrops in the Sound that caused the tide to split and swirl in dangerous eddies, a menace to shipping even in calmer weather.

It must have seemed like a lifetime to the crew as the SS Lonsdale slowly fought her way down the Jack Sound, with the constant pitching, thumping and groaning throughout the very heart of the ship. Then disaster struck. There was a tremendous bang and the ship lurched in an uncontrolled manner. The steering gear had fractured under such unaccustomed strain and the SS Lonsdale was suddenly just a helpless hulk. As the storm-lashed cliffs of Midland island came inexorably closer those six souls within her realised the hopelessness of their situation.

The details of this story did not unfold until much later, but Father and Mother - knowing these treacherous waters well - had guessed at much of it, and their reaction to the situation was typical of those who lead seafaring lives. Although by this

The Wreck of the SS Lonsdale, en route from Belfast to Milford Haven, driven by the storm on to the rocks on Midland Island. She had replenished her coal bunkers off Martins Haven beach, but the storm and the Jack Sound proved too much for the old lady, and her propeller shaft broke under the strain, with inevitable consequences.

time the coastguards had requested the launch of the Angle lifeboat, Father and Mother both realised that there would be a considerable delay before it could reach the stricken vessel. There was not a moment to lose, and of course they had to get out there and provide whatever help they could.

Grandfather, who was staying with the family for a short holiday, had by now joined them. There was a shared sense of extreme urgency and near desperation at the thought of the Lonsdale's crew attempting to reach safety in those stormy and very unfamiliar waters. Father, Mother and Grandfather quickly headed for Martins Haven beach to check conditions there, and decide how best to launch their boat.

Fortunately the haven itself was partially sheltered from the full force of the gale by the headland. Even so, it was still difficult for each to hear the other's words in the general maelstrom. The three of them set about launching their sixteen foot open boat, with the little outboard motor on the stern, struggling down the beach and pulling the boat over greased sticks to within a few feet of the pounding waves. They paused momentarily waiting for that precise moment when a superhuman effort would be needed to ensure that the boat entered the water and was sucked outwards. The wrong moment and a wall of water could hurl it back on to the beach, and completely swamp the boat.

At Father's shout the boat hit the water, halted for a fleeting second and then mercifully, helped by the receding undertow, gained momentum. This was probably the moment of greatest peril. Father had to make his way to the stern of the boat as quickly as he could, whilst Mother and Grandfather had to struggle with the long oars to turn the bow seawards. Everything depended on that little engine springing to life on the first pull of the cord.

Those few moments must have seemed like an eternity and all three were already aware of the mass of water that was, within just a few moments, swilling around their ankles in the bottom of the little boat. Against all the odds, the engine sprang to life on the first pull and they were underway, moving out as quickly as they were able under the lea of the protective headland. Survival now depended on superb seamanship and great courage, and the belief that the Almighty would provide each one with the strength to see them through.

On the way out, full advantage needed to be taken of each sheltering rock and promontory, and every eddy and backwater needed to be utilised to the full in order to provide relief from the force of the enormous waves. The flying spume stung their faces until they were numb, and all the while they were wondering at the fate of the crew of the Lonsdale. They would surely not have left the refuge of their ship, however helpless and frightened they might feel.

On board the Lonsdale it was a frightening scene. By now the old ship was being relentlessly battered against the rocks at the bottom of a cleft in the tall cliffs on the North side of Midland Island. She was already holed at the stern and starting to settle at a drunken angle. The huge seas pounding her unmercifully, she settled even further on to the reef of jagged rocks which ran out underneath her amidships. Some years earlier, within living memory, this reef had already claimed the SS Molesley and the lives of some of her crew.

For one fleeting moment the skipper wondered whether it would be possible to reach the safety of those rocks, so near and yet so far. The powerful seas swirled and pounded the ship again and again, and each time there was a jarring thump as the vessel grounded repeatedly on to the rocks below. It did not take more than a few moments to realise that to abandon the old ship in her death throes was now the only course to take, however frightening the prospect.

Captain Hegarty's mind was in an emotional turmoil, His ship was dying under the battering that she was receiving and he decided that his place was with his stricken vessel. He refused the entreaties of his crew to join them in the ships lifeboat as he ordered them to abandon ship without further delay, else they would all perish in the attempt.

The ship's lifeboat was a small but strong seaworthy craft and the lowering from the derricks was quick and surprisingly trouble-free, undoubtedly due to the sharp angle of the ship and an unexpected lull in the wind just at the crucial moment when the lifeboat hit the water. By this time, as luck would have it, the Jack Sound was also just on the turn, and the sharp chop of the waves in the lea of the island was temporarily easing.

As the exhausted crew desperately pulled away they could just see the outline of their poor stricken ship lying at a crazy angle amid the white waters at the bottom of the steep cliff. Captain Hegarty could also be seen clinging to the rail, still defiant on his stricken ship. Suddenly, in the distance ahead of them an unmistakable noise could be faintly heard, the noise of a motor which came and went with the force of the wind.

It took a little while for the two small boats to locate each other in the stormy waters, but they eventually came together and between them managed to attach a tow line, much to the relief of the exhausted Lonsdale crew. It was then that Father discovered that the Captain was still on his stricken ship and refusing to leave. He decided very quickly that there was only one thing to do.

Suffice it to say that Father was a powerful and persuasive man and eventually managed to persuade Captain Hegarty that his vigil in his dearly loved ship made no sense at all. With tears streaming down his face the Captain abandoned the ship that had been his life for so long. The two small boats later struggled into Martins Haven with their exhausted and numbed crews. It was almost a surprise to see how those waves pounding the beach seemed suddenly much calmer and unmenacing compared with those they had just left out there behind the headland.

It was now dark as they approached the beach, but fortunately the District Officer of HM Coastguards had arrived and was able to guide the boats in with his powerful searchlight. All thanked God for the feel of solid land under their feet, and for a mission safely accomplished. The Angle lifeboat, which had been launched earlier, could now be informed that the crew had been saved and the services of the lifeboat were no longer needed.

Two days later the sun shone in a clear blue sky and the water lapped gently on the Martins Haven shore. The only reminder of the last few days was the abnormally high bank of pebbles after being thrown up at the top of the tide, and the large lumps of seaweed now scattered on the foreshore, that had been wrenched off the sea bed by the relentless pounding of the waves.

On the beach stood a small group of people dressed in slacks and sweaters, chatting amongst themselves and occasionally glancing out to sea, when around the headland came a little boat with three people sitting relaxed in the stern - Father, Mother and Grandfather returning from checking the wreck of the Lonsdale. As they slowly approached the beach, ready to leap ashore, they were greeted by what were now recognisable as reporters and photographers.

After much questioning and photographing, one of the

Mother, Grandfather and Father - after checking the shipwreck serveral days after the storm had passed.

reporters turned to Mother and said "Did you know that it is exactly 100 years ago to the day that Grace Darling also went out to rescue the crew of nine off a foundering ship?" The fame that came to Mother in the national press was quite astonishing, with the press christening her Grace Darling the Second. The National newspapers and Pathe News had a field day.

The formal record of this 'incident' in the official Coastguard log for that watch simply reads as follows:

'Re. SS Lonsdale. V in C (Volunteer in Charge) *Wooltack Point has rescued crew of six in his motor boat, and landed them at Martins Haven. Angle lifeboat has been recalled by St Annes Head. Vessel is on North side of Midland island, and crew were taken off on account of the vessel's dangerous list'*
And later: *'vessel is holed, rudder gone, propeller damaged'.*

The Lonsdale lifeboat was eventually given to us and proved to be a useful addition - seen here with Grandfather leaping ashore ahead of disembarking some visitors to Skomer.

And so back to today

As we approached Skomer North Haven those memories of our life on Skomer kicked in again. If we had been but two months earlier we would have been met by an almost overwhelming scent of bluebells wafting down over the water from the shoreline above. Thousands of puffins, razorbills and guillemots would be all around us, in the air and on the water, and the constant bird calls would be almost overpowering. One could also observe the occasional shag or cormorant standing on the promontory and flying low across the water, and visitors arriving in Skomer North Haven could not fail to be totally captivated by the puffins flying back to their cliff-top burrows to feed their young with the sand eels in their large orange beaks – over 10,000 puffins can be found on Skomer during the breeding season.

Our arrival in North Haven today – we were delighted that there were still some puffins on the water to welcome us. One can just see our old landing beach on the right, and the WTSWW warden's accommodation - built since our time – situated just back from the cliff top above the North Haven.

While it was a little sad that we had just missed that experience, we were none the less delighted that there were still quite a few puffins swimming around. They must however always keep a weather eye open for any sly predatory Great black-backed gull swimming nearby which, if the slightest opportunity arose, would grab a puffin to make it release its catch.

As we came closer to the shore, we could now discern a steep railed path up the cliff from the disembarkation point. Undoubtedly this was an easier way of disembarking than that of old, but I couldn't help missing that exciting feeling when the keel of our open boat ran up the shingle and we leapt out to help the visitors to disembark.

This new path up the cliff eventually joined the original track at its first hairpin bend, and it was here that we were made very

Arriving with another group of visitors in 1949 - Mother poised to leap on shore in Skomer North Haven. We had this boat built to our own specification in a local boatyard in Dale. On one occasion - on a calm day - she carried 25 marines over to Skomer - an experience not to be forgotten. In those days 'Health and Safety' considerations were not the preoccupation that they are today, and no one felt the need to wear lifejackets.

A heavily laden dray on its way to the North Haven beach being pulled by Prince - led by Father. A typical load could include empty Calor Gas cylinders to be replaced, rubbish for disposal, items requiring specialist repair on the mainland, and items bound for market such as rabbits, flowers and gulls eggs when in season.

welcome by the WTSWW resident wardens Eddie and Bee, and some volunteers. After a short briefing on their role in protecting the integrity of the island, and in supporting appropriate research, we briskly set off up the path.

In the days when we farmed Skomer we had three main modes of transport, apart from shanks' pony of course. We had a pony called Billy, who had been on the island for many years after being taken there in the boat by my grandfather. We also had a Shire horse called Prince, a truly majestic animal, who was mainly used for pulling a sled dray between the North Haven beach and the farm house. He was also used to plough the first furrows - using a deep Wilmot plough - when bringing the fields back to cultivation, and for drilling furrows when planting early potatoes.

Getting Prince over to Skomer set us a major challenge, but eventually the decision was made to swim him across by the side

Haymaking with family and my Llandovery College friends during the school holidays.

Prince and Billy drilling for potatoes - Father in charge with me helping. The ground could be very stony, and major breakages from striking large boulders were not uncommon. A capability for us to be able to carry out a wide range of repairs, without resorting to mainland help, was essential.

of the boat. That worked very well for the first part of the journey, but inevitably he tired, stopped swimming, and rolled over to have a rest. This acted like a drag anchor on the boat! Suffice it to say that, after several very sticky and hair-raising moments en-route, Prince eventually strode heroically out of the water on to the North Haven beach. When we sold Skomer, we left Prince and Billy to end their days peacefully on the island. They kept each other company for quite a few years until the day Billy was found dead in the lea of a large rock. Around his body was a well-worn circular path - Prince had clearly mourned the loss of his long-time friend.

Our third mode of island transport was a Fordson tractor. It was mainly used for the various cultivation tasks after the initial ploughing, and for powering a large circular saw for sawing large timbers that were often washed ashore after gales. Transporting this tractor to the island in our open boat was yet another major

Our Fordson tractor - which had to be split into its parts to enable it to be transported to the island in a small open boat. This involved constructing a wooden tripod with pulleys so that the parts could be raised and, when the tide came in, carefully lowered into the boat – with the reverse process at the other end.

challenge. However, this was overcome by the construction of a tripod hoist on Martins Haven beach, which enabled us to hoist the tractor in separate parts and lower them into the boat which then floated when the tide came in. At the other end, the tractor had to be reassembled on North Haven beach before being driven up the path. Time and tide were both critical - there were only six hours available to reassemble the tractor, and drive it off the beach to safety before the tide came back in.

Today, as we walked up the path from North Haven, with the vivid memory of our Prince with his dray in my and my sisters' minds, we passed one of the old lime kilns that I had often explored as a boy, which dated back to the late 19th century. In days long gone the coastal barges would bring in limestone and anthracite coal to the beach below. Horses with carts would be driven alongside the barge, which lay on its side on the beach, and the coal and limestone would be loaded into the carts and

Mother and me – taking the lazy way to the North Haven – Grandfather leading Billy pulling the dray. Tina - as usual - looking for a cuddle.

One of the two old Lime Kilns -The boat delivering limestone and coal was beached in the North Haven, and the cargo was then offloaded and driven by horse and cart up to the lime kilns. The slaked lime was used on the land, and for mortar for building walls.

driven up to the lime kilns where the coal was burned to slake the lime in order to produce fertiliser for the fields. The lime was also used in mixing the mortar needed in building stone walls and farm buildings. We did not use those kilns in our day and any fertilisers that we needed had to be laboriously brought in to the island in 1 Cwt sacks, following their delivery to Martins Haven beachhead.

We pressed on up the path past the Harold Stone, which is a rock pillar about two metres high, about which there has been no information concerning its origin. The island does in fact have many iron age remains, comprising hut circles and signs of cultivation, and I was led to believe that on the Neck an ancient burial site had been discovered some years before our time.

As we continued up the path towards the farm we noticed that there seemed to be much more bracken around than in our time. Noticeable also was the fact that there were far fewer

The Harold Stone – of uncertain origin and still a mystery.

shearwater carcases on the path, although we weren't sure why. The Manx Shearwater is very much a Skomer presence - it is one of the largest single colonies in the world - and particularly noisy at night. They are birds of huge stamina – I remember that in 1938 a shearwater was ringed on Skomer and was caught again only ten days later in South America.

At the top of the path, before we entered the first field, we stopped at Bread Rock and I reminded everyone that life on an island can be very different from the idyllic conditions of that day. We had lived on the island over many summers and winters, come rain or shine, storm or calm, and each had its own particular challenges and rewards. Even the challenge of really rough and alarming storms can be very exhilarating as the seas pound the cliffs, raising clouds of spume, and a wind so strong that it literally almost sweeps one off one's feet.

As for the rewards, they often came from the flotsam and jetsam, which provided surprisingly useful items for we island dwellers used to having to make-do. During the war I well remember grey cube-shaped life rafts, which had been washed off ships, coming ashore. They often contained tins of Pemmican and chocolate slabs, as well as tins of water - a veritable treasure trove for the young island dweller.

But enough of that while we stand in the sun reminiscing on this day in July 2015. I harked back to an occasion in the winter of 1948, when a gale had sprung up, preventing contact with the mainland. We were all in the house, where Mother and Annie Lloyd – our home help of many years – were cooking our evening meal, when my sister June hit her head violently while dashing through a passage under the stairs. Worryingly she developed severe muscle spasms, and it was clear that a doctor was needed. But how to arrange that in the prevailing conditions, with no radio communications of any kind and in the midst of a howling gale?

We knew that, in times of dire need, a distress fire should be lit on Bread Rock, but we had never before needed to put it to the

An ancient habitation in Skomer North Valley. Many ancient remains can be clearly discerned in various parts of the island.

test. However, it was certainly worth a try, so Father and Arnold - our elderly rabbit catcher – set off for Bread Rock with sufficient fuel to make a large fire, and a torch with which to flash distress signals. In the gale force wind it wasn't too difficult for them to get a raging fire going, which was soon seen by the coastguard on Wooltack Point. They also flashed the word 'doctor' in morse code, as well as the standard distress code SOS, but unfortunately the coastguard's skill at reading morse was about as rudimentary as those sending the message, and he alerted the St. Davids lifeboat without mentioning the need for medical help.

The lifeboat arrived within the hour, but was in great danger of approaching too close to the rocky shore. To prevent any possibility of harm to the lifeboat in those extremely turbulent conditions, Father struggled out to it in our small boat to explain the situation. The crew radioed to Milford Haven for a doctor to come, and arranged for him to be collected from Martins Haven.

A shearwater and chic in an exposed rabbit burrow nest, a sight not normally visible. One of the largest Shearwater colonies in the world can be found on Skomer.

Gull and chicks in nest - a commonplace Skomer sight.

He eventually arrived on Skomer some hours later, to find that June's symptoms were thankfully subsiding satisfactorily.

It is interesting that previous inhabitants on Skomer had fashioned their own signalling system to communicate with the mainland. In the late 1800s the island tenant had erected a mast on Spy Rock - could this have been our Bread Rock - with agreed signals as follows: One hoisted heather bush meant that a boatman was needed. Two heather bushes that a blacksmith was needed, and three heather bushes that a doctor should be brought. How so very different it is today, with mobile phones and Air/Sea rescue helicopters - no more need for heather bushes!

A Peregrine Falcon on our tennis court - recovering from an injury to its wing – It was rescued by father after it had flown into a telegraph wire on the mainland.

A Peregrine falcon with its well developed chick

Razorbills on a Skomer rock outcrop - only here to breed, then back to sea. They mate for life, and only lay one egg a year.

Kittiwakes on the ledge at The Wick.

Guillimots nesting on ledges near the South Haven – note that the egg is shaped such that it will not roll off the ledge.

And so to the family home

Our party then moved on from Bread Rock, and across two fields towards the ruins of our old home in the centre of the island. When Grandfather had bought the island he extensively modernised the farmhouse, much of which had its origins way back around 1840. He installed electricity throughout the house and outbuildings, supplied by a Lister generator through a bank of commercial vehicle batteries, as well as a domestic water supply pumped using a small JAP engine from a spring near the North Pond. He had a first floor veranda built along the full length of the south facing front of the house, and also brought his beloved billiard table which he installed in the East Wing.

What for us, in those days, was a very comfortable family

Storms and neglect after our departure in 1950 soon ravaged our old home - so sad to see the roof stripped of its slates, and the front veranda totally collapsed. It can be seen that only our old farm implement shed, and our converted chalets off the front lawn, are still left with a sound roof.

home, is now a sad ruin, with the roof blown off in a gale in 1954. As we entered the gates in front of the house it became only too clear how, over the years, the winter storms have ravaged our lovely old home, leaving only the walls standing; although it still retains a certain charm under its ivy cladding. The WTSWW staff have rejuvenated the lawn in front of the house – indeed it looked rather better than in the days when we had a tennis court there! Some of the barns have also been restored to provide useful accommodation and facilities for visitors.

Looking after visitors to the island had formed an important part of our lives, and we met many interesting people. Famous names that stick in the mind include Princess Juliana of The Netherlands, Lord Montagu of Beaulieu and Sir John Hunt of Everest fame. Ornithologists and photographers were regular guests in our home, and included Professor Grimes, Peter Scott, Eric Hosking, Ludvig Koch as well as many other well known names from that era. Father and Mother both treated their

Our dining room on Skomer in 1949 - ready for our ornithologist and academic researcher guests. They would sleep in the chalet bedrooms that we had converted in the old barn nearby. Every time that I look at that old Benjamin Prinz oil painting nowadays, I am taken back to that scene of our dining room on Skomer.

June doing the milking - no machines in those days.

conservation responsibilities very seriously indeed, and a new 'sighting' always generated much excitement.

They did however take serious issue with what they considered to be truly cruel and barbaric practices by some so-called wildlife 'experts' of that time. For monitoring purposes, metal tags were attached to seals' flippers - not an easy task – and this had to be carried out using sharp tools. Father was deeply incensed at seeing how much blood was shed in this process, and at the apparent cruelty of this practice. Thankfully, today, I believe that a spray dye is used to mark seals, which is clearly a much more humane process.

We next went into what used to be our old dining room, now open to the sky. There were a number of helpful displays providing some historical facts about the island and its inhabitants, including our family of course. Behind the dining room lies our old kitchen, and nearby was the dairy where during the school holidays my sister June or I would have the task of making butter

Our family home on Skomer in 1948, with Valerie going for a ride on Billy. Grandfather had the veranda built on to the South facing front of the house, but the ironwork protection eventually proved to be no match for the salt laden winds on Skomer.

in the barrel churn. The churn had to be turned at a relatively slow but even speed and, as the butter was gradually formed in the churn, one would hear the thump thump as it fell from end to end in the churn before the buttermilk was drained off. It was a regular chore that neither of us much minded doing.

My most vivid memory of the kitchen was an occasion during WW2, when we called into the house on one of our many checks on the island. On the kitchen table was a saucer containing a bar of soap, which was still wet and which had obviously been used in the past few minutes. Clearly we had disturbed someone, most probably a German submariner (some days earlier Mother had spotted a submarine sheltering on the surface near the north shore). We returned hurriedly to the mainland to call the police, who eventually arrived fully armed, but no one was found and the mystery remained.

Today we wandered around the house surrounds, starting

with the kitchen garden on the west side of the house where I remembered one of the only two trees that existed on Skomer. This was an apple tree that Grandfather had planted in the shelter of a high wall which protected it from the salt laden winds that were a regular feature of winter storms.

Proceeding around the east side of the house we noted the ancient bacon curing ovens - dating from about 1700 - set into the east side of the house, next to the outside wall of our old billiards room. We never used those curing ovens and, although we had bred pigs, we cured our bacon in brine.

On an island one has to be pretty self-sufficient and, in addition to the pigs, we kept cows for their milk and for making butter, chickens and turkeys and a flock of geese for eggs and the table, and sheep for their fleeces. And of course rabbits were in very plentiful supply all over the island; an eclectic mix of colours and types – white, black, angora, as well as the usual grey.

Rabbits had been introduced to Skomer over seven centuries ago, and have been exploited by virtually every owner and

The rear farmyard in 1948, with an old horse roundabout and driving gear, that had been used for driving the grain processing in the adjacent barn, via a shaft in the barn wall.

I was always slightly nervous of our geese.

their tenants since then. Indeed, the sale of rabbits was a useful addition to our income, as was the sale of early daffodils that grew in profusion in beds along the front of the house. Gulls' eggs were also in great demand by the best hotels in London, and we would send quantities via the Great Western Railway from Haverfordwest.

When collecting the eggs we were careful only to collect from nests where there was just one egg – any more would indicate the possibility of at least one being addled. We were never too sensitive about collecting the eggs of the Great black-backed gulls - they were possibly the fiercest predators on the island, as evidenced by the many hundreds of Manx Shearwater corpses that littered the paths every year. The gulls would certainly think nothing of attacking if one ventured too close to their nest, and that could be quite a frightening experience. It is interesting that their threatening behaviour in some of our coastal towns now seems to have become a real problem. (For us, pricking their eggs to prevent hatching was quite an effective, although somewhat laborious, control.)

Our breeding livestock included beef cattle, which were mostly Herefords, and Kerry Hill and Suffolk sheep, flocks of which were confined to grazing on The Neck. The shepherding of these could be an extremely hazardous task, with sheep looking for good grazing frequently having to be rescued by Father from the ledges and gullies on the cliff edge – at considerable risk to life and limb! I remember Father telling me that he always positioned himself on the outside edge of the ledge, because the sheep would be less likely to slip over the cliff edge - in its mad dash to escape - if he stayed on the outside of the ledge. Those were the days when 'Health and Safety' did not figure as highly in everyday life as it seems to today.

On our visit to the house it was most surprising to find the little wooden bungalow on the east side of the converted barn still fully intact. During the war years, Father and I used to stay

Sheep on the Neck - being herded to the sheep pen to be checked for fly blow and maggots, and the young rams to be castrated.

Sheep shearing - with June providing the power. The shorn fleeces were stuffed into a very large sack, made by sewing together about 6 to 8 ordinary sacks, which was then taken to Martins Haven for collection by lorry.

overnight in that bungalow when visiting the island on rabbit hunting trips. Our stay was never likely to be a restful experience, because of the continuous cacophony from the shearwaters nesting underneath the bungalow floor. But it was always a worthwhile experience, and our evening meal of winkles, picked off the rocks in North Haven on our way up, was an enjoyable repast at the end of a long day.

Our rabbiting dog 'team' consisted of Tina, a lurcher who was very fast at catching the rabbits dazzled in the torch beam, and Trudie a spaniel who would retrieve them from Tina and carry them back to us. They worked together as a well drilled team and, once a sack was full, Father would hide it under the nearest rock outcrop, to be collected, with the many other sacks, in the early morning.

Today, after looking at the site of the old horse roundabout at the back of the South Barn - which had been used in the very old days to turn the corn grinding stone and later to drive a basic threshing machine inside the barn - we retired to the high rock behind the yard. We relaxed over a nice picnic lunch, reflecting on what an enjoyable morning it had been. Sadly time was not really on our side though, so we decided that a walk to The Wick, to see the kittiwakes and some remaining puffins on the opposite bank, would be the wisest course.

We followed the well-marked path to The Wick, and dallied for a while to enjoy the bird life on the ledges and banks. The view down The Wick inlet was quite dramatic, with 200 foot high cliffs on one side. These dramatic cliffs, with their hundreds of ledges are virtually covered with sea birds - Kittiwakes, Razorbills, Guillemots, to name but a few.

The steeply sloping banks on the opposite side of The Wick provide a natural habitat for a vibrant Puffin colony. That slope

Father doing the odd spot of rabbiting, with ferrets and Tina – a centuries old Skomer tradition. Pegged nets were put over all adjacent rabbit holes, and the muzzled ferrets would drive the rabbits out of the burrow and into the pegged nets. Tina would catch any that escaped.

is also a great vantage point from which to view the heavily populated ledges opposite and some family members managed to get very close to the puffins, much to the excitement of the grandchildren. We then followed the path back to the North Haven, and being somewhat early for our return boat, went down the path to the beach to relax while we waited.

The gentle lap of the water against the boat's sides, the constant background bird chatter all around, and a couple of good books, all provide a thoroughly relaxing break from life's chores for June and Valerie in our little carvel-built boat called Puffin.

Valerie and me, with Trudie and Tina, our constant companions.

An unlikely alliance - Lady Ming and Teddy.

Our 1946 help - Back Row are Cousin Brindley (who was there to help us to convert a barn into chalet bedrooms), Joseph Koch (a German POW) and Artie (our handyman). Front row are Father, Mother and me.

Our night time base during the war when we were rabbiting overnight - not a quiet night for us with the loud and incessant underfloor Shearwater chorus that continued unabated until daybreak.

June was always ready to take on an orphan.

Some final recollections

My very first thought when we reached the beach was to look for my name on the concrete winch base; I had idly marked it in the concrete when Father and I had constructed the base all those years ago. I was only just able to discern it in the front right hand corner, although I am sure that no one else would recognise it. That was quite an emotional moment for me.

North Haven Quay and landing beach with two boats safely hauled up - the 'gateway' to Skomer.

And as we looked out across the North Haven at a lone sailing boat lying at anchor, I was reminded of the French fishing boats that occasionally visited the North Haven to seek shelter when weather conditions from a southerly direction were threatening. We would take Annie Lloyd, our Welsh speaking housekeeper, out to the French boat. It appeared that the Welsh and Breton languages were so similar that each could understand the other, enabling her

View of the North Haven from The Neck, showing the track from the quay that zig zags up to the centre of the island, past the lime kiln in the middle distance, and on to our island home about half a mile inland.

to indulge in a spot of bartering - some freshly caught rabbits for lobsters and langoustine. This was a culinary treat for we island dwellers, particularly when we had so little time to set our own lobster pots. Dear Annie. We all loved her dearly.

On this day in July I reflected on the fact that this beach had always been the sole landing point for the island, and was therefore the main channel through which absolutely everything flowed. As such, it held many memories. There had always been a deep sense of anticipation whenever I was going to the mainland on an errand, or returning after a rough crossing and looking forward to getting back home; but most of all I was reminded of the incredibly difficult challenges and tribulations associated with this place.

Just stop and reflect for a moment. If you order a ton of coal on the mainland, it is delivered by lorry to your home coal bunker. For Skomer it was delivered to the top of the approach to Martins Haven beach. Twenty 1 cwt bags of coal would then have to be carried on our backs, down the beach to our boat, and across the water to the North Haven beach, where they would be lifted out of the boat and carried up the beach to the quayside. The twenty 1cwt bags would then be loaded on to the dray, to be pulled by Prince for nearly a mile inland to the house, where we could finally unload it into our coal bunker - just one example of the huge amount of extra time and effort that was called for in everyday life on the island.

That same hard slog applied to every item of the big weekly shop in Haverfordwest, and to the constant stream of needs for the farm. And if we had a special building project, which was not unusual, it would pose its own transport challenges. At one point an ex-military amphibious DUKW landing craft had to be used to transport very cumbersome and heavy building materials to the island.

But perhaps the most dramatic challenge on that beach was when very large fattened cattle had to be taken to the mainland for sale. The verdant pastures of Skomer always produced the very topmost grade of animal, beasts so large that there was always a danger of them holing the bottom of the boat. This challenge called for special measures to be taken, the first of which was to bring over to the island several strong men from Marloes village.

The targeted animal had to be corralled up against the side of the specially modified open boat that we used for this purpose. Two of those men would then slide strong planks under the beast's belly, resting one end of the planks on the side of the boat. A well timed heave would pitch the animal into the prepared fern bed in the bottom of the boat, where it would quickly be roped down so that it could not cause harm to itself or the boat. Compared to the cattle, the transportation of sheep was a doddle, but it still imposed an additional task that mainland farmers did not have to contend with.

Father told me the story about how on one occasion, after the boat had been beached overnight on the mainland, a rat had leapt out from the fern bedding in the bottom of the boat upon its arrival back at Skomer North Haven. Fortunately diligent trapping over the following days caught the rat which was found to be about to produce young. A threat to Skomer's vermin-free state was thus narrowly avoided.

Some of the unhappiest memories that this beach evoked for me were those of my return to boarding school at the start of each term. I simply hated the very thought of leaving family and home, and was always overjoyed when we were stormbound for a week or two at the start of a new term. Living on the island did of course mean that boarding school for me and my sisters from the tender age of six years old could not be avoided. Of course my school friends from Llandovery College loved coming to stay during the holidays - particularly useful at harvest time - and the Girl Guide Troop from my sisters' Convent School in Fishguard also looked forward eagerly to their Summer Camps on Skomer.

It was an especially sad time when Grandfather, who in his later years lived in Dover, had cancer and returned in 1949 to his beloved Skomer to die. He was very weak and in a great deal of

My sisters' Girl-Guide troop regularly came camping on Skomer - with Sister Pauline in charge. I remember that she acquitted herself really well on our tennis court, in spite of her voluminous habit.

pain, but was determined to spend his last days on the island that he loved so dearly. I can so understand how he felt, because this unique place does cast a spell that one never really shakes off. He now lies in Marloes churchyard with Grandmother.

And then there were the happier memories; the joy of returning after a long absence, the wonderment of the raucous bird life all around, watching the seals rearing their young on the beaches. And yet at times one could still find complete tranquillity in all that frenzy, and be in another world entirely. What powerful, and often conflicting, memories.

Three generations relax for a moment on the beach in North Haven.

Bedding down calves into the soft fern bed that we had put into the bottom of the boat - on their way to Skomer for fattening. Much needed help was provided by volunteers from Marloes village.

Positioning over 13cwt of beef, in order to tip it into the boat for the return journey to the mainland after fattening. The fattening process on Skomer consisted simply of grazing cattle freely off the verdant vegetation on the island until they attained the topmost grade (Super Special) in the marketplace - which they invariably did.

Four strong men, two planks and one good heave does the trick.

And quickly roped down in the soft fern bedding in the bottom of the boat. This boat was a large old ship's lifeboat, which Father had converted specifically for carrying cattle by removing a central thwart (seat) and installing a special engine mounting.

A docile cow enjoying the trip - a happy passenger under a comforting hand.

Sheep were a far easier proposition.

And finally, leaving the boat at Martins Haven – ready for road transport to the farmers market in Haverfordwest.

Two Atlantic Grey seals enjoying the surf on a Skomer beach, before the start of the breeding season in late Summer/early Autumn.

A seal pup suckling on a North Haven Beach - in September 1948. Pups are fed by their mother for 3-4 weeks, during which time they can triple their weight, while their mother loses much of her fat reserve.

Seal pups are born with a thick coat of fur, which keeps them warm until they have gained huge fat reserves, after which they are then ready for swimming lessons by their mother before she leaves them to fend for themselves.

Prince and Billy – who were really close friends right up to the end. We left them both on Skomer after we had sold the island, not wishing to put Prince through another exhausting swim back to the mainland. They roamed their island home together for many years before ending their days there.

A sad departure

And so, after such a wonderful day, we went back up the path to thank our kind hosts, and to embark for the return journey to Martins Haven. The water was relatively calm and the journey uneventful – in contrast to many crossings that I remembered from the past, particularly those in the winter months when the conditions were most challenging.

The strength of the wind and of the tide, and how the two interact with each other, are undoubtedly one of the biggest challenges to be faced in island life. However, when both of those are least in evidence, dense fog could make the journey even more nerve-wracking. Father always kept an old ship's compass handy (it came off the Lonsdale I think) for those occasions when fog was likely. In such challenging conditions we knew that our journey home would be really difficult, with a visibility of no more than ten yards in the dense swirling mists and the fog horns on St Anne's Head playing tricks on one's sense of direction.

During the war years there were many winter trips to the island when I was really glad to be safely back in the warm in Martins Haven Cottage - such as after a couple of days of catching rabbits on Skomer. On our way back from the island I would often be huddled in the stern of the boat, with breaking waves on our quarter, and concentrating on steering while trying to avoid the freezing driving spray. Meanwhile Father would be sitting amidships gutting the rabbits and throwing the paunches into the sea.

Upon our arrival at Martins Haven we would carry about 200 gutted rabbits up to our garage to hang overnight, ready for Tommy Reynolds from Marloes to collect for market on the following day (Tommy would carry virtually anything in his large old Austin saloon - 200 rabbits one day, and the bride to her wedding the next!).

Father used to say that the sea is a good servant but a bad

An occasion that I remember with fondness - chatting with Father on Martins Haven beach on a sunny day, with the water lapping the shore, while we wait for a group of visitors to arrive.

master, and he was so right. At the start of this foray through my memories, I mentioned Jack Edwards who lived in Marloes. Jack was a quiet unassuming man, and a highly competent seafarer in whom all could place complete trust. As such he was a great help to Grandfather during his early years on Skomer. In fact Grandfather owed his life to Jack.

On this memorable occasion, Grandfather needed to take supplies, including coal, to the island and was accompanied by Jack, who was always ready to help. They set off from Martins Haven but the weather conditions rapidly deteriorated soon after leaving. After battling against an ever increasing head-wind they eventually had to abort the attempt, but by this time had lost any opportunity to make landfall again at Martins Haven. As darkness fell, and the storm continued unabated, they could only run with the wind, their sail in complete tatters, hoping against hope to find shelter.

In the stormy darkness they eventually found themselves passing the Stack Rock in the south east corner of St. Brides Bay. This was their very last opportunity to find shelter, and they only just managed to row in under the lea of the Stack Rock. Holding that position in such turbulent conditions was well-nigh impossible, so they threw a sack of coal, tied to a line, over the side in the hope that it would act as a drag anchor. Unfortunately, after a short time, the sack broke open on the sea bed, and had to be replaced by the second – and last – bag. This bag eventually suffered the same fate, and the two totally exhausted men could only try and maintain their position as best they could in the turbulent waters under the lea of the Stack Rock.

Meanwhile, the emergency services had been out all night scouring the coastline, and Father and Mother had virtually given up all hope of ever seeing Grandfather alive again. It was not until the following morning, when the worst of the storm had largely abated, that someone in Little Haven village thought that they could see a boat out near the Stack Rock. Both totally exhausted men were safely brought ashore, and so another small, but not untypical, episode in Skomer's history ended happily.

In a gale force South Westerly wind there is no shelter available on the long inner shore of St Brides Bay, other than Stack Rock, and it goes without saying that Jack Edwards and Grandfather were extremely fortunate to survive their long and exhausting ordeal.

The Stack Rock, close to the inner shore in St Brides Bay, provided the very last opportunity - as darkness was closing in - for Grandfather and Jack Edwards to find shelter from a fierce on-shore storm. They miraculously survived the night, and emerged totally exhausted as dawn broke. (Photo by courtesy of Rachel Mullett - Pembrokeshire Moments)

And so to the end of a wonderful day

After we had disembarked at Martins Haven on that lovely July day, with so many memories and emotions still welling up inside me, what were my feelings as I reflected on the wonderful day? I realised of course that at the centre of island life as we remembered it, were our father and mother, Reuben and Betty Codd. They are no longer with us, but this story is really theirs, not ours.

Their story was about two young people from completely different backgrounds, who found themselves in this wonderful but extremely challenging place. Those backgrounds naturally engendered different personal priorities and expectations of life, which were hard to reconcile. But in the early years their love of this island, and their deep sense of personal responsibility for safeguarding and nurturing such a unique place, provided the common bond and shared tenacity of purpose needed to farm on Skomer and bring up a family on this remote island.

Farming is a tough enough life at the best of times, but on a remote island it poses huge additional challenges, and the realities of island life were such that one was seldom able to stop for a moment to enjoy the sheer magic of life in such a place. Time for occasional relaxation, such as a game of tennis or a swim in the South Haven, was indeed a rare luxury.

But we did have some wonderful times on those rare occasions when one could just shut out the everyday pressures of keeping on top of our daily chores. One could lie stretched out amongst the sea thrift on the cliff edge and seemingly in another world entirely, and being totally absorbed in the rich variety of bird life all around, or simply sitting and watching the seals sunning themselves on the beach below. That was sheer magic.

And on rare occasions in a warm Spring or Summer, one could observe Basking Sharks cruising around the North haven feeding on plankton. They are massive creatures, up to about twelve metres long - the second largest fish in the world - and the word Shark tended to make one nervous about being too close. But they are really 'gentle giants' and not to be feared.

What a cocktail of wonderful life enhancing experiences to reflect on and, even though there was little time for such things, those simple experiences made all the hard grind of island farming life so worthwhile.

As we return home and approach the North Haven, Tina shares our sense of anticipation that we are nearly home at last. How could I ever forget that picture!

But back to those chores; the reality of that island farming life was the constant backlog of urgent tasks, most of which needed someone highly competent in a wide range of practical skills. Those essential skills encompassed blacksmithing, joinery, animal husbandry which included shoeing the horses, building construction, catering for visitors, and providing facilities for research projects, in addition to dealing with all manner of emergencies. The routine replenishment of essentials from the mainland also filled a great deal of one's time. And so it went on......................

The Codd family thrived for many years on that hard, but very satisfying existence, but the never ending pressures to survive commercially, together with the constant challenges of island farming which was increasingly commercially uncompetitive, eventually proved too much for one family to cope with on their own. Father's and Mother's very different expectations of life also played an important part in their final decision to leave Skomer, hence the sale of the island in 1950 and the end of an era in Skomer's farming history.

And as I come to the end of my recollections, I stop to ponder on what are my most enduring memories of growing up in our island home. The elements obviously played an important part in our lives, and these could be both ferociously challenging or serenely calming. The former would include memories of those bitterly cold and stormy winter passages across the Jack Sound, and the struggle up the beach with heavy loads in the freezing cold weather, barely able to feel one's hands.

A Skomer puffin - fresh back from a fishing trip. An abiding and fond memory of such a characterful and lovable bird which mates for life. (Photo by courtesy of Mike Alexander).

Then there are the memories of those moments on a calm and sunny day, when Father and I whiled away the time relaxing in the boat at anchor in the North Haven, waiting for the last group of visitors to appear. The peaceful gentle lapping of the water against the boat, with not another human sound to disrupt the magic of the moment, is for ever etched into my memory. It was simply idyllic.

The beautiful orange glow of this glorious sunset over Skomer provides an evocative and beautiful end to many a long but exhilarating day on the island. (Photo by courtesy of Mike Alexander)

There are also deeply personal memories of Father and me sitting chatting in the sun on the path edge overlooking North Haven, while he reminisced about old Marloes characters and their exploits, how much he loved our island home, and about his worries and expectations about Skomer's future.

But I suppose that my most evocative memory has to be that of approaching Skomer North Haven on a calm and sunny day, with the incessant clamour of the birds all around - in the air and on the water - and the wonderful scent coming down over the water from the acres of bluebells above the haven. And amidst it all was the sight of those wonderfully captivating puffins, the thought of which now still makes me feel so homesick. I can only say that there is still an emotional void in me that I know can never be filled.

Our family group visiting Skomer in July 2015. Sadly our son Justin and his family were unable to join us that day.

Back row (left to right) is me, my wife Christine, Valerie, June's partner Tom and June. Middle row are daughters Louise and Emma and son-in-law Noel. Front row are grandchildren Emily, Daniel and Izzy.

And what was the most important conclusion that we took away from our family's return trip to Skomer in July 2015? – It was that we should rest assured that the Wildlife Trust of South and West Wales is proving to be a worthy guardian of this unique place, the place that the Codd family did their very best to protect and nurture over so many years, and the place which now forms a wonderful heritage for all to enjoy in perpetuity.

Sadly though, there is an ever growing challenge to the integrity of a unique natural habitat such as this. Pollution by our increasingly industrialised world, and the pressures from a populace which expects the 'right to roam', combine to form a significant threat which needs constant vigilance to protect our natural inheritance. The Wildlife Trusts are the guardians of that habitat and deserve every possible support in meeting that challenge.

And so I come to the end of this reflection on a life that is no more. Father would be simply thrilled that so many of the trials, tribulations, and joys that we experienced while we were the guardians of such a wonderful place, have now been recorded for posterity.

I am however only too conscious of how difficult it is to convey the full emotional impact that assails those who are fortunate enough to have lived in such a magical place, but I hope very much that I have been able to convey sufficient of that magic to encourage others to experience it for themselves.